# THE ANSWER

James Nelson

**The Answer**
Copyright © 2019 by James Nelson
Published in the USA by Covenant Consulting

ISBN (978-0-578-22136-6)

Printed and bound in United States of America

## Acknowledgments

First and foremost, I want to thank God for seeing me and believing in me, despite what He knows about me. I give all credit to Him for His guidance, patience, and love.

*Thank you* to my beautiful wife, Wendy Nelson. She is an amazing woman, mother, and friend. She has been an advocate since the beginning, even when I didn't believe in myself. She is my rock and not afraid to get in and fight with me. Babe, I am grateful to God for you.

*Thank you* to my children – James (JR), Imani, and Jade for your consistent love and support. I am proud of all of your accomplishments and I am waiting with anticipation for what you will conquer next. I am doing my best to lay a foundation and set the stage upon which you can stand. The sky is the limit and nothing is impossible for you.

*Thank you* to my parents, Bishop James and Bessie Nelson, for being my biggest cheerleaders. You have pushed, covered, and loved me through my worst times. I am grateful to God for sparing your lives so you can celebrate and reap the benefits of my best times.

*Thank you* to my brothers and sisters – Anthony, Janice, Jonathan, and Jason. You are my sounding boards, support, and a safe place. Your love and respect has helped me to soar. I am forever grateful. There is nothing like family.

*Thank you* to Tiara. All of your hard work has really been a vital part of my success. Please know that it has not gone unnoticed. I pray you develop these skills into an enterprise that can bless others.

*Thank you* to Bishop T.D. Jakes – my spiritual father, mentor, and gift from God. God brought you into my life at the right time. I would not be writing this book nor be the healthy person I am if you were not present. Thank you for seeing greatness in me and mining the diamond in the rough. On May 26, 2019, you allowed your platform to be my *answer* and launchpad into my next. In honor of my gratitude, I dedicate this book to you.

*Thank you* to Pastor T. Renea Glenn, for being a gift to me and my family. You've encouraged, prayed for, and poured into me for years. Now we are starting to see the fulfillment of the word spoken over my life. The kingdom is better because of you.

*Thank you* to my sister, Pastor J. Denise Ray, for pushing me to write this book. You spoke into my life, challenged, and held me accountable. You constantly reassured me the world needed to hear what I have to say.

*Thank you* to my entire staff – especially my executive assistant, Natasha Edmonds.

*Thank you* to all who support me and receive the gift that is *me*.

# Table of Contents

# Foreword

Bishop James Nelson, Jr. is a beloved friend and brother in the Lord. As is characteristic of authentic friendship and fraternity, it is common for our conversations to cover a wide array of subjects. I have thereby come to know and respect Bishop Nelson as a true Renaissance man, a man of many gifts, talents, and areas of knowledge. And yet, I am continually amazed at how the subject of faith becomes the common denominator and lens through which every other subject of discussion is viewed. Indeed, one does not have to know or talk to Bishop Nelson long to learn that he is a man of great faith in the all-encompassing, predestined purpose, plan, promises, and prevenient grace of God.

Such faith is reflective of more than secondary or book knowledge, but is reflective of personal experience. It is the kind of faith that the prophet Habakkuk and the Apostle Paul describe as a lifestyle: *The righteous shall live by faith*. It is the kind of faith that the inspired biblical author James identifies as having been authenticated and developed through testing: *The testing of your faith produces patience*. Similarly, in *The Answer*, Bishop Nelson brings an array of existential, theological, philosophical, and testimonial themes together to encourage and empower others to trust and embrace the predestined plan of God. And in reading *The Answer*, one is essentially accepting an invitation to join us at the dinner table or on the telephone and glean from the priceless life-lessons and wisdom of my friend and brother.

*The Answer* is a book about self-discovery, holy and healthy self-acceptance/esteem, and sacred service to others. Via personal transparency, Bishop Nelson makes it clear that all are divinely intertwined. Personal destiny and corporate destiny are inextricably connected. Even when painful, our experiences in life are purposeful and ultimately designed to be productive and beneficial for ourselves and others, thanks to the prevenient grace of God. Prevenient grace is divine favor that precedes human experience to manifest destiny in the due course of time. But *prevenient* grace also calls for *responsible* grace, which is the responsibility God gives us to share the grace we have received with others who are in need. In other words, God has graced each of us to serve as an incarnate answer to someone else's concern or prayer. Thereby, it can be said that *The Answer* is a product of responsible grace, inspired by God and penned by Bishop Nelson to nurture our faith in the great things God has prepared for His children. So turn the page, join me at the metaphorical dinner table, and let's glean from the faith-nurturing wisdom of my friend and brother!

**– Dr. C. Guy Robinson**

# Introduction

*"Row, row, row your boat. Gently down the stream. Merrily, merrily, merrily, merrily. Life is but a dream."* That is how life feels sometimes. Sometimes, the dream is beautiful and at times the dream feels like a nightmare. Life is complex, a full multiplex of everything. Life is an adventure that is only enjoyed if it is lived. Fact is, what's most encouraging and inspiring is the life we live has been strategically designed and customized to be the stimulus and example for someone else. Most people selfishly focus on personal impact, instead of realizing the occurrences that have happened in life – both good and bad – have been the catalyst used to be the solution for someone else. You cannot take someone to a place you've never been, nor can you show what you have never seen, or even testify about what you've never experienced. The design of life is to be lived to become a model for someone else.

There are some people who are not aware of this and need help in discovering the real meaning of life. There is an old song that says, "If I can help somebody, then my living shall not be in vain." Your life has meaning and value, and can impact someone else whether you are aware of it or not.

*Discovering Destiny* is the name of the game, and because I've struggled with this in the past, it has become one of my passions. I enjoy helping people discover their destiny. I do not believe destiny is fate nor chance, but is preset and yet to be discovered. It is also my belief that we play a role in our own destinies and whatever direction we choose will dictate the outcome. Let me explain. We can make choices that impact the direction of our lives. For example, whether I decide to rob a bank or if I choose to go back to school, both are choices with consequences. However, whatever my destiny is, it will ultimately be realized – whether behind bars or behind a desk. I know from personal experience that there is a predetermined outline for our lives, as well as people we are trusted to reach and impact. Now, the *how* may vary, but I am convinced it is still supposed to happen.

This book is birthed from personal experiences and lessons I have learned. I desire to bring light to the fact that we are someone's answer. What does it really mean to be the answer? The answer can be a person who was destined to become the solution to someone's problem. It can also be a resource, place or direction, beacon of light in darkness, or even an umbrella on a rainy day. The answer can be any variation of things. Here is the theory behind it: anytime God wanted to help or do anything in the earth, He always did it in human form. When He needed an intercessor, He looked for a man to do it. When the world needed a Savior, God sent His Son in human form. According to scripture, when it comes to blessings and reciprocity, the Bible says men shall give into your lap in "good measure, pressed down, shaken together and running over". Even when Cornelius prayed for an answer, Peter was sent to him. You are what somebody has been praying for. Your experiences are positioning and qualifying you to help someone. This book is purposed to help you uncover purpose from life's pain and provide strength within your struggle.

After reading this book, it is my ultimate desire for you to:

1. Develop an understanding of how your journey was necessary to become who you are. This empowers you to not be bitter from what you have been allowed to endure.
2. Know that all things have reason and play a part of a bigger picture.
3. Find healing and wholeness from all previous pain and trauma that resulted from your experiences.
4. Have courage to be the answer you are.

Now, let's begin the journey to discover how you can be somebody's answer. The world is waiting on you.

# Chapter One
## The Bigger Picture

As I sit gazing into the blue skies overlooking the earth and reflecting, my mind hones in on the thought that everything is impacted by something else's existence. Everything that exists does not exist outside of itself, but was made to exist within a system of other existing things. Take the earth for instance, it is a beautiful entity with life sustaining ability. The earth is so expansive and vast that new parts and aspects are still being discovered and explored. The earth is home to over 7 billion people with an atmosphere that is conducive for human life, plant life, and vegetation. Its mountainous peaks are breath taking and its bodies of water are overwhelming. It is full of hidden treasures and heartwarming experiences which leave lasting impressions.

The earth is so vast that it takes days to transport from one end to another. Yet with all of its characteristics, splendor, and independence, the earth is a part of a bigger system. The earth does not exist alone. Earth is a part of a planetary structure called the solar system. The solar system is comprised of the sun, eight planets, more than 150 moons, millions of asteroids, and billions of stars. The solar system's movement is set by the rhythm of its planets being in constant rotation around the sun. Yet, as vast as the solar system is, it's a part of a galaxy known as the Milky Way. Everything flows together to become a part of a system. Planets and stars may exist on their own, but they're not isolated. The earth was created for us to live on, but not created to be on its own. The earth is independent, yet interdependent. It needs the sun for energy and the sustainability of life.

On earth, there is another system named the ecosystem. The ecosystem is a biological community of organisms and their environments. Trees need the soil they are planted in and the birds need the trees planted in the soil. There is a flow of energy and interconnection in the ecosystem. One group depends on and feeds off of another. Another example is within food chains. You have what is called producers and consumers. Here is a sample food chain flow within in a grassland. Grass is a producer, a mouse consumes the grass, a snake consumes the mouse, and a hawk consumes the snake. Everything is interconnected, intertwined, and interdependent with something else.

You and I are no different! While we have our independence, we are very much interconnected, intertwined, and interdependent. From conception to birth, the cycle, the interaction, and collaboration produces life. We could not get here on our own. Life is a process and a system all of its own, depending on the action of each participant. While your mother and father's interaction was the catalyst to kick off the cycle of life, there were other extenuating factors to bring them together. Their coming together triggered the next stage of collaboration and interaction resulting in the production life. Our existence was dependent on another, whose existence was dependent another. In creation, God made systems and not isolated entities. All things are interconnected. We all have a unique role to play and are members of a bigger picture. It is with this understanding that we are able to progress. Your existence is necessary to fill a role for the one connected to you. This is what gives life meaning – finding your fit. It is purpose. It is the bigger picture.

## You Matter

Some people live life making random decisions, wandering aimlessly because they have not found their role, their space...their purpose. Purpose is the driving force that motivates us to go, endure, push and deliver. Purpose makes me get up every day. Purpose is what has brought meaning to my life. I understand that I have a fit. I see the bigger picture – my existence is necessary to complete the system God has created. My being is designed to impact and save someone's life. My children would not be who they are without me. The church I pastor would not exist without me. The countless lives that I have impacted and won to Christ would not be changed without me.

The truth is, I didn't always feel this way. In times, I didn't always have a sense of purpose and belonging. As a matter of fact, I felt like I didn't matter and the world, my church, and even my family would be better off without me. I had not grasped the concept of the bigger picture and how intertwined my life was with others. I was blinded by self-pity and overwhelmed with what I believed was failure, not realizing that there were no wasted moments in life. Similar to the earth and the eco-system, I was born to fit and contribute. I had a unique role to play. I hadn't come to grips with the fact that I was both a producer and consumer. It didn't occur to me that my being out of place could throw the whole system off.

When you grow up as a member of a bigger system without an understanding of your role and the importance of your role, you just simply exist. You live from moment to moment. For a period, that is what it was for me. I didn't have a hard or bad life, and I was blessed to grow up with both parents in our home. My siblings loved me and I was gifted in multiple areas. God blessed me with great opportunities at a young age. And for all intents and purposes, life was good. I watched my father gradually take us from apartments in the ghetto to spacious single family dwellings in the suburbs. However, with all of this, life still felt empty. I struggled with depression most of my life. I didn't live life on purpose, for purpose, or with purpose. I just simply lived. Suicide was easy for me to entertain and eventually attempt. I was hard on myself, and the feeling of failure and letting others down drove me to thoughts of ending it all. I hadn't come to an awareness of what my life was purposed to be. I was an answer. What's interesting is looking from the outside, it seemed I had it all together. No one would assume all this was going on. I was suffering with high-functioning depression. It is possible to function in day to day activities, celebrate the success of others, experience what others dream of, and yet still feel empty, unfulfilled, and irrelevant. I starting preaching at the age of twelve and began ministering in various places on my own by the time

I was thirteen. God blessed me to travel extensively – which included to other countries – and allowed me to preach on national platforms, all before the age of twenty. I had a strong family foundation and support system. You'd think I'd made it, but there was just one issue – I was still struggling with identity.

Without purpose, failures aren't opportunities for learning. When you don't know your fit, failure can feel like pressure. When you add failure to depression, the stress of trying to make everyone happy can be the perfect cocktail for suicide – or so I thought. All I could do was think of ending it all and how much better life would be in my absence. I want to be clear, I am not glorifying suicide, nor am I encouraging anyone reading this to try it. Some would even suggest that suicide is cowardly. Suicide is the option that Satan presents because he knows the blessings and results that come with you striving to live in your purpose. Understand this, death is not an option before its time. If you keep living and pushing, you will eventually have your epiphany, opening your eyes to who you're destined to be and what you are destined to accomplish. By sharing my story, I want to show you how deceptive a life without purpose can be. You'll be made to feel like you don't matter and you're irrelevant. Without purpose, you will have no sense of meaning and direction – you will just live in the moment.

This is what happened to me. I had no hope. Already feeling like a failure – to add insult to injury – my suicide attempt failed and got me a week long hospital stay. I couldn't even get that right! Can you imagine the frustration of feeling like a failure and even your attempt to end the cycle of failure failed? What do you do when literally nothing works? Welcome to my world! But in reality, everything that was happening – failures and all – were a part of God's plan for who I am today.

All of that's good to know now, but at that point, I was completely unaware that I mattered. Truth be told, I was hypocritical. I preached to others what I was not living and believing myself. I preached "all things work together for good", but I really didn't believe it. I only viewed my life from an isolated perspective with me as the focus. I didn't view myself as a part of something bigger. All I could see was what was right in front of me. I only saw from my own restricted view. One's perception is their reality, hence the need for other's views. Having the input of others helps to create a panoramic view of life verses only a singular perspective. Isolation endangers and is a secret weapon that limits and even debilitates. Mental isolation is as harmful as physical isolation in a social context. Think of isolation like this, in *The Art of War* by Sun Tzu, one tactic suggested is to attack by stratagem. The idea is to isolate your enemy as a means of offense. Sun Tzu writes, "The next best [strategy] is to prevent the junction of the enemy's forces." Isolating your enemy keeps them from being empowered by connection to their allies. Therefore, in the context of a person's perspective, isolated views or thoughts becomes the prison to limit one's outlook on life and self. There are times when the angle needs to change to give a different perspective of the same picture. I was in mental isolation and could only see from the lens from which I viewed the world.

## A Higher Vantage Point

Perspective determines perception! Growing up in school I was always intrigued by geography. Hearing stories about Columbus discovering America, the earth's circumference, and all the continents that spread across the world captured my attention. However, what I found to be most interesting was the map of the earth. I found the earth's layout to be amazing! Land gathered here and there surrounded by bodies of water, the strategic placement of each continent, the countries in their perspective places, and the coloration of land mass water with blues, greens, and browns had me awestruck. I was intrigued and desired to one day see the world as it was laid out by map designers.

There was one prevailing question constantly plaguing me. Where did the artist get this concept from and why didn't I see this when I traveled? What I saw didn't match what was displayed in school. Every year, my family would travel all across the United States from the east coast to the west coast and back again. For the life of me, I could not understand where they were getting the information from for the map.

That all changed one year on Easter. I was thirteen years old and my favorite uncle, the late Apostle Floyd E.

17

Nelson Sr., lived in San Diego, California. Uncle Floyd, as I affectionately called him, was one of my childhood heroes. He was one of the major inspirations and influencers in my life – along with my father – prompting me to begin a life of ministry. Here I am, thirteen years old, about to see one of my favorite people in the world. I was so excited for the voyage I was embarking upon. For a thirteen year old boy, this was more like an adventure. This was going to be the best Easter ever! I was on my virgin voyage in the air. I had never traveled by airplane before. I was used to traveling by car and even by bus, but never by plane. I was nervous and excited all at the same time. I didn't know what to expect. After all, I was taking this trip alone. I remember the roar of the engines as the plane picked up speed zooming down the runway while lifting off the ground. Just like that, we were airborne and I was on my fantastic voyage from Maryland to San Diego. I was in awe as I gazed out of the window watching objects that were huge and massive diminish in size the further from the ground we rose. Over time, my awe of flying subsided and the captivation of my surroundings calmed. As I settled in for what felt like an endless flight, I began to make a connection. It was in that moment where what I saw in person matched what I'd seen in my geography class. I realized where the creators of the map got their information. I saw the distinguishing outlines, separating the land from state to state and I could plainly see the color scheme portrayed on the geography map.

The lesson to be learned here is at times looking at something can require a change of perspective. My previous vantage point only allowed me to see things from ground level, however, at 35,000 feet in the air, everything looks different. The map designers had a different vantage point from what I was used to seeing. I had been looking at a piece instead of looking at the whole picture. Everything I had seen and admired about the earth now made sense because I saw it from a different vantage point.

It becomes difficult to discover purpose and see how you fit into the bigger picture when you're looking from ground level. Could it be you don't feel like you matter because of your vantage point? Maybe the angle from which you are judging is limited. It took a plane ride for me to see the connection between perspective and perception. H.M. Tomlinson states, "The world is what we think it is. If we can change our thoughts, we can change the world." Limited view equals limited perspective. If my perspective is limited, then my perception will be as well.

The trouble with viewing from a limited perspective is you never get all the facts. Just as I was confused about the map because I could only see the earth from my grounded view, that's what it's like when making decisions. You can't regard yourself as a failure, being worthless, sad, and never able to do anything right when you only have one perspective. I rendered a verdict on my life without having all of the evidence. It was a wrongful conviction and premature judgement because the defense – God – had not finished presenting His case. I still had life to live and great things to accomplish. I still had children to raise and businesses to run. I still had a church and a book to birth as part of my purpose. Suicide became palatable for me because of the view from which I saw the world. I am so glad I failed miserably at suicide – all failure is not bad.

## The Jury is Still Out

It's important to gather all of the facts before coming to a conclusion. Life is still in the process of being lived and there's so much more for you to accomplish. It is not helpful to quit and give up at the first sign of trouble or challenge. All of the things I thought were life ending, all of the situations I thought were too overwhelming to deal with, all of the mistakes I thought I could not recover from – as I lived on, I found they were not as they seemed. I soon realized that once you grow, the obstacle that once looked big and scary begins to shrink. What I once looked up to I now look down on. I gave up too soon and too easily, and I didn't have to. Let's not misunderstand the fact that I made major mistakes and dealt with some of the consequences of those mistakes in public for all of the world to see. I have had entire organizations black ball me. I have experienced people trying to sabotage my ministry. I've been humiliated through repossession and having utilities cut off. I've fought through marital issues and family dysfunction. Nevertheless, I kept going, growing, and living. I understood the proverbial saying, 'the jury is still out'. This means that no conclusion has been reached. In other words, my destiny was still being unfolded.

I'm living proof that there's another move to make, even if you don't see it from your current vantage point. There's a story about a man visiting an art display, when suddenly he comes across a picture of a chess game with the caption 'Checkmate'. Everyone thought it was a great piece. While his companion moved on to the next piece of art, the man stood there and stared at the painting. After a few minutes of staring, he called to the management of the establishment and insisted that the caption needed to be changed or the painting had to be done over. Not understanding as he gazed over the painting, the manager asked, "Why?" The man simply explained to him that the king chess piece had another move. Those who are not expert chess players would see the painting and take it as is. But the person with experience in playing chess understands how the game is to be played and understands how to win with strategy. Learn from me: do not conclude, pack your bags, and go home when it is only intermission, because the jury is still out.

**Diamond in the Rough**

How you see yourself is greatly influenced by your view. Your view is shaped by previous experiences, education, environment, and exposure. These things become the lens through which we view the world. They shape our values and ideas. They influence our thoughts, dictate our feelings, and ultimately control our behavior. I hope by now you are starting to open up to the idea of elevating your angle to get a different view. You may be as I was, a diamond in the rough. There was treasure in me but I couldn't see it through all of my other stuff. I didn't see my worth and value, nor did I comprehend the impact of the gift called *me*.

Diamonds are fascinating, mesmerizing, and very costly. They are signs of love, wealth, and commitment. Diamonds are naturally formed out of carbon and are considered the hardest, natural material. These precious stones are also considered 'a girl's best friend' because of their significance and status. Diamonds are valued by their clarity, cut, color, and carat. But more than just looking pretty, diamonds have several other uses. According to the Natural Museum of History, diamonds conduct heat five times faster than copper, can pass or block electrical currents, and can endure extreme temperatures and chemical exposure. Sharpened diamonds are often used as specialized drill bits in producing microchips and semiconductors. Who knew a piece of carbon could do so much? In its raw state it looks like just another mineral. You have to know specifically what you are looking for when you see one. Diamonds do not come easy. Their process begins about 100 miles deep within the earth before they are brought to the surface. The natural carbon is put under intense heat of 752 degrees Fahrenheit and under the extreme pressure of 434,113 pounds per second. I believe it's their development process that causes diamonds to be so durable. People are like diamonds – once fully developed, they are beautiful, durable, and full of potential, possibilities, and capacity. Like diamonds, our process starts deep within and has to be put under heat and pressure in order to bring out clarity and brightness. One's value is equal to the carat of a diamond, and varies from person to person. This is why comparison is an unhealthy practice, because as diamonds are unique, so are we. Also, as diamonds are found in the rough and raw stage, as are people.

I was the diamond in the rough being developed into the answer I am today. I was not aware at the time that life's issues, mistakes, family dysfunction, and public trials were nothing but heat and pressure to bring out the purest form of greatness that was locked inside of me. I had to endure those things in those times in order to become who I am today. I had to be able to withstand that in order to ensure I can stand now. It started deep within, with raw feelings and emotions. I was full of capacity and possibility. I just wasn't aware of it. I perceived that the pressure of living up to people's standards, being a preacher at twelve, and trying to fit in were really helping to shape me. I did what many have done, I tried to quit by aborting God's process and finding an easy way out. The day I first attempted suicide, I remember waking up angry at God for letting me live and face the fact that my attempt failed. However, today I am overjoyed that God knew and saw what I did not see and kept me alive to help anyone that hears my message, whether spoken or written. I mattered back then and I still matter now. I had purpose but just needed perspective to enhance my perception. Now today, I proudly and confidently know I am the answer.

Your life has more meaning than you've imagined and your worth exceeds your sense of understanding. Your existence is of the upmost importance, but you won't realize it if you're afraid to elevate your mind. I realized there was so much more and I was just getting started on my road to discovery.

# Chapter Two
## No Wasted Moments

What Defines You? What really brings meaning to your life? What are the perimeters that shape your life? How do you determine success? What is considered the sum of who you are? These are real questions many are plagued with. Some people judge themselves by trivial finite material things. We measure who we are by our popularity, using Instagram and Facebook 'likes' as measuring barometers. We determine success by financial gain, and we compare ourselves to what is portrayed on television and through social media. Most of the tools we use are superficial at best and really don't have any meaning. How many followers you have doesn't convey your real influence. Your bank account is not a true indicator of your success, nor does popularity dictate if you are truly loved. You can have money and still be unhappy. You can have a significant other and still not feel loved. You can have food and not be full. There are individuals who have plenty of money and popularity, lost it, and then gained it all back. Was it the money that made them successful or was it something greater and intangible?

For years, I constantly compared myself to everyone around me. I looked at material possessions and popularity status. As a young preacher, my focus was always about getting into the biggest pulpits and filling up my ministry calendar. When I looked at my friends and others I envied, I created my own unspoken competition in my head. As a healthy man now, looking back, I can see the unhealthy tangibles I used to define success in life. It's amazing how maturity and life's experiences can teach you what really matters.

## Healthy Self-Worth and Self-Value

'I'm more than that!' This is what I had to tell myself to help create a new healthy mindset. I admit that I was a bit superficial and got sucked into the hype of having things as a form of status. I thought if I could acquire certain things, if I could go certain places, and if it was known that I knew prominent people, then my acceptance level would raise and my self-esteem would raise right along with it. I knew if my accomplishments were broadcasted, I would be loved and accepted by everyone but mostly, I'd love myself. Boy, was I wrong! My master plan backfired greatly. All it did was cause debt, add stress, and weaken what was already a diminished view of myself. You can't build self-worth and value off of the opinions of others. People can be fickle and change like the wind. Look at Hollywood and the entertainment industry. There are stars and artists who can be on top of the world today and blacklisted tomorrow. People buy music based on popularity and likability. The populous will shut down on you if you make one decision they do not like according to their own preference, and it doesn't have to be illegal or immoral.

As unhealthy as that mindset was, it's what I wanted. It's what was paraded in front of me and it became the social standard. For someone immature, easily influenced, and struggling to discover who they are, it is very simple for them to be swept away by the powerful currents of trying to gain acceptance, status, self-worth, and popularity through superficial means. Then it happened – God sent me a Moses to lead me out and show me the way to the promise land. God loved me so much not to let me squander any longer by connecting me with someone who understood where I was but discerned where I was to be. This is none other than my spiritual father, mentor, and now friend, Bishop Thomas Dexter Jakes. Sometimes it takes an outside, unfamiliar voice to awaken the sleeping things that are lying dormant inside, but were there all along. The crazy thing is, I thought I was alright until I found out that I wasn't. I thought I was good until I became aware of how unhealthy I was. It wasn't Bishop Jakes telling me, but rather showing me how unhealthy I was. He effortlessly personified wholeness, which in turn exposed my unhealthiness. Since we are being honest here, I knew I had a few issues but my goodness, was I really so bad? Yes, I was. I was living in deception, I was basing decisions on faulty data, and I was comparing myself to individuals who in some instances were just as bad – if not worse – than me. **There is nothing worse than ignorant arrogance!**

My transition brought transformation, causing transcendence. I got a glimpse of healthiness and I began to mature. That is a powerful combination. Maturity is powerful because it helps filter the unimportant and the unnecessary; and healthy becomes the standard to attain. Here is something else I learned, none of the things I valued really mattered. Transition was my process, transformation was the change, and transcendence was my end game. All of this is a direct result of a renewed mind. My outlook shifted when my mind changed. My definition of success changed with my mindset. What I valued shifted, and who and what I thought I needed changed with my mind. As a result of transformation, I was able to transcend. A transcended life is one that is independent of the standards that normally restrict and define others. A transcended life is one independent of preconceived concepts and social expectations. When I transformed, what used to affect, define, and influence me lost its appeal and power.

Here is the secret to my transformation. There is a verse in the New Testament of the Bible in Romans 12:2 that reads, *"Do not conform to the pattern of this world, but be transformed by the renewing of your mind. Then you will be able to test and approve what God's will is—his good, pleasing and perfect will"* (NIV). The key in this verse is the renewing of the mind. Understanding the plan for my life can only come through transformation. Transformation comes by means of mind renewal. Everything hinges on mind renewal. Renewing the mind is not merely adding information to an already cluttered brain. Rather renewal is displacing old thoughts with new thoughts. It is a mental purging of sorts. It is deprograming and reprograming. It can be likened to a corrupt computer that needs to be cleaned and ridded of all of its programs and then rebooted by downloading updated software. Part of the reprograming was on how I perceived myself. Now, thanks to my renewed mind, I have a healthy view of myself. I have confidence I've never had before. I am no longer consumed with what others have or do not have. The biggest thing is, I no longer allow people to set the parameter for my identity and acceptance.

The sooner you come to this realization, the better you'll be. Cars, clout, clothes, and cribs will never make you YOU. You are defined by more substantive and qualitative things like purpose, passion, and destiny.

## What Really Matters

What I have come to discover is success, impact, and true influence cannot be measured by material superficiality. There is something more meaningful, but yet intangible. It is not based on numerical data and algorithms. Purpose is an intangible which is simply what you were created to do. If I start a business and make millions of dollars but never fulfill my true purpose – which is my *why* – am I really successful? Have I really made a difference and an impact?

Everyone alive has a reason for existing. All humans have a *why*. It is the reason you were born. For man, purpose came before production. Let me further explain. The Bible records the creation of man and the purpose behind man's creation. God took six days to initiate the creation of the world. On the first day, God created heaven and earth. On the second day, the sky was created. On day three, plant life and dry land with all of the continents, islands, and mountains came into existence. On day four, the heavenly bodies and stars including the sun and the moon were spoken into reality. On the fifth day, marine life and flying creatures were created. On day six, God creates all living creatures and man. What is not often detailed is how God has an agenda for the creation of man. God needed someone to watch over what He had already created. Creation was made with the ability to reproduce itself but God would not allow rain to fall, which would trigger this growth. The Bible tells us that God wanted someone to till, maintain, and oversee what was created. **Man had a purpose when he was formed.** He didn't simply come into existence without finding reason. There was a *why* before there was a what. Finding out *why* is what changes the game. Understanding *why* adds value and meaning. Finding your *why* is not the end but the beginning of discovering your purpose.

Existentialism suggests that we determine our own development through acts of will. The issue with that is no one created themselves. God is the true creator and He always had a plan for man in place before creation. God predetermined the purpose and destiny of each individual before there was an embryo in their mother's womb. Let me be clear, we do have free will and the ability to make decisions that affect our future and development, but God still expects us to fulfill the purpose we have here on earth which brings true meaning to our lives. Purpose has to be discovered, realized, and embraced. Therefore, it is not totally left up to us to discover what our purpose is. This is something I call divine orchestration, where God intervenes and sets up moments for individuals to discover purpose. The challenge with these divine moments that cause great pause is the fact that those moments are not always pleasant. Sometimes it is through tragedy and loss, other times the moment is wrapped in failure and mistakes, and then there are instances enveloped in detours and delays. Sometimes it is disguised as hurt, pain, and heart break. I never knew life's hardest moments had the potential to be times of prolific awakening, strategic development, and empowerment. Prolific awakenings are revelations that change and transform. It is information I was previously unaware of that once I received, altered my thinking and caused me to never be the same. Strategic development is intentional growth and planning. Empowerment is power and authority to do what I previously was unable to do or perform.

**Divine Chaos and Ordered Falls**

We are a society of skepticism and excessive scrutiny. We are more apt to believe in chance and fate than destiny. People are more intelligent with internet information readily available at their fingertips. Everyone believes they have an idea about which direction their lives should take; and with this thought, they outline, strategize, and plan their path. The detail we miss is the fact that man does not determine his own purpose. We have input but we do not have a final say as to what our *why* is. Purpose has to be discovered and revealed. Based on my own experience, I believe God ensures purpose and man have a collision. I also learned that purpose is time sensitive and does not need to be known until the specific time when it is to be acted upon. That does not mean one cannot discover their purpose before it's implemented. It simply means that the moment when your purpose unfolds, you'll know.

This is where I believe sovereignty comes into play. The magnanimous nature of our purpose is too critical to overlook. In the book, *To Be a Mouse*, by Robert Burns, he states, "The best-laid plans of mice and men often go awry. No matter how carefully a project is planned, something may still go wrong with it." God will not allow purpose to be missed or overlooked. While I do not subscribe to the saying 'God made me do it', I do however believe deity influences decisions. Purpose, or a person's *why*, is not really about them but about those who will be impacted as a result of their *why*. As the answer, people are depending on you to accomplish what you were born to accomplish, be who you were destined to be and go to where you were predetermined to go. It is imperative that it happens.

If I failed to reach purpose and comprehend my *why*, many people – from my wife and children, to thousands all over the world – would be shortchanged and left with a deficit. No one can be 'me' better than I can. My son, who is my namesake, looks just like me with some of my characteristics, but can't occupy the space tailored for me. I had to occupy the space tailored for me, and still am required to do it. I'm not writing this book as a conclusion but as a beginning. Heaven knows how essential purpose is and what lives are at stake as a result, so heaven gets involved to guarantee you discover the revelation of purpose. Divine chaos and ordered falls are my way of communicating to you that the devastation, loss of employment, upheaval, and even the consequence of a one-time decision are all used as a part of God's plan. He uses this to position us to receive understanding of what our *why* is.

There is a story of a man named Joseph, who is allowed to experience betrayal, rejection, false accusation, slavery, imprisonment, and abandonment. I am impressed with Joseph who did not allow all of his negative experiences to make him bitter. Instead he recognized heaven had orchestrated a divine strategy to bring awareness of his *why*, which enabled him to execute his purpose. He came to the understanding that he was right where he was supposed to be. He further understood that all that was done to him was intended to be evil, but God orchestrated it for good so he could save lives. Divine chaos and ordered falls. Sometimes heaven has to intervene to get us to where we need to be in order to bring us to the place of prolific awakening, strategic development, and empowerment.

What I found was my response and attitude toward this divine chaos and these ordered falls determined what I took away from those moments. Please fight the urge to become embittered and resentful of your specific journey and process. Understand as Joseph and I did, it was and is necessary to position you to discover your *why*.

## It's Up to You

When purpose is involved there are no wasted moments. Everything has meaning, whether you see it now or later.

Each triumph, success, failure, mistake, sickness, excitement, disappointment, frustration, hurt, gain, and advancement are all filled with meaning designed to shape our lives. Together, they produce the person you are now and who you are destined to be. What draws out the positivity of these pregnant moments is our perspective of those moments. It is like I said in the previous chapter, your view – which is nothing more than your perspective – positions you to see either a part or the whole picture.

Why are we able to see good and learn from some situations and not others? What caused you to grow from this tragedy verses what made you become bitter from that disappointment? Why could you get past that but not this right here? It is all about beliefs and values which shape perspective and influence. This ultimately results in behavior and response. Discovering one's belief helps to explain how they view and respond to events in their life. What hinders or helps what we see rests solely upon our value system. What we believe and prioritize directly influences how we see what we see. Perspective is the vantage point from which I see a thing. Perception is how I interpret what I see. If I wear glasses with red tint, everything I see will have a hue of red. Seeing things in red is my perception, but looking through a red lens is my perspective. The only reason I interpret everything as red is because of lens I have viewed it with. Life is the same way. Each moment and circumstance can be interpreted both positively and negatively; my takeaway is based on which vantage point I view it from. Therefore, if I am to extract prolific awakenings, strategic development, and empowerment from all that I endure, my beliefs have to be so aligned.

Beliefs and values are developed over time and are shaped by exposure, education, experience and, environment. These basic things help to formulate what a person believes and values. Another essential term to understand is principle. Exposure, education, experience, and environment crafts a person's principles. Principle is what drives what we do and how we respond, and determines the character of who we are. When life happens – and life does happen to us all – our response to what happens determines what we gain from the situation life has allowed. Events are permitted to happen to us with a predetermined outcome called purpose. Principles govern behavior and behavior regulates what our takeaway is from each event. The discovery of purpose is equivalent to baking and cooking. For instance, there are many different ingredients needed for various types of meals and cakes, but having ingredients doesn't make the meal or cake. The meal or cake manifests once the proper ingredients are correctly mixed and the right temperature is applied for a specified amount of time. It takes everything you have and will deal with to fully equip you to be the answer you are.

**He Won't Leave You Broken Like That**

Returning soldiers have heightened awareness as a result of the after effects of exposure to traumatic experiences. This is known as Post-Traumatic Stress Disorder, or PTSD. What is often overlooked is how traumatic experiences are not just wars but sicknesses, divorce, loss of loved ones, mistakes, unsuccessful careers, sexual violation, and many other things. Even once the event is over, there are after affects and residual occurrences directly related to what happened. The common objective is healing, but the deficiency with healing is it only deals with the issue itself and not the ramifications of the issue.

There are many scriptures that reference Jesus healing individuals from their specific issue, but periodically you see Him say "be made whole". Wholeness not only addresses the immediate issue but the effects of the issue. A perfect scenario is the woman who had a blood flow for twelve years. When she touched Jesus, the blood flow stopped. Jesus realized what happened and after a brief conversation, He tells her to be whole. **The immediate issue was blood flow for an extended time**. Blood flow for a woman was not uncommon as it is a natural thing, but to have it last twelve years was problematic. Customs of that time separated women from society and family until their monthly cycle passed. There was equal lack of both social and intimate interaction. Additionally, the cost of medical attention was economically impactful. Jesus' command, "Be made whole", caused every effect the woman suffered from because of the blood flow to be addressed.

Everything is needed as a part of the formula to equip and qualify you to be the answer you are; nevertheless, all of those things may come with potential side effects. I want to encourage you: every side effect will be addressed. There are painful things I suffered that had their own side effects. Some I was aware of and others I was not, but the good news is God will find a way to make sure every need is met – whether emotional, spiritual, or physical. God will not leave you broken. He will make sure you are healthy and whole so you can be effective in your relationships with others. You will be a healthy answer. Take refuge in knowing all was not for naught and you will be made much better after it is all over. Here is to all the healthy healers.

# Chapter Three
# The Awakening

Enlightenment...awakening...epiphany. Each of these terms center on the same concept, which is coming into a place of greater knowledge and understanding. Life is full of teachable moments that are designed to educate us and ultimately evolve us. Humans are built to constantly adapt and evolve. Some ascribe to the theory that man started out as an ape and became a man. We know this as evolution. I do not personally ascribe to this mindset, as I believe man was made in the likeness and image of God. I believe man was not inferior but has always been superior to all other created things. Man was made with power of will and choice, and was created with capacity, potential, and unlimited possibilities.

The mind of man is far more advanced than any artificial intelligence or any computer ever created. Those who study the mind are constantly intrigued and baffled by the intricacies of the brain. The brain is multilayered and multifaceted, complex but yet simple. God spared nothing in the design of mankind. He gave us the ability to speak, make choices, have free will, express emotion, store and retrieve data, and demonstrate creativity. Most importantly, we have the ability to house the Spirit of God Himself, setting man apart from any other existing creature. The brain has the ability to adapt, compartmentalize, and comprehend data. Understanding the intricacies of the mind's composition and it being the central control center for the human body helps one realize the awesomeness of man. Man really is the express image of the thoughts of God. If you want to know what God thinks of mankind, take time to fully explore who you are. Here is a principle for consideration: everything produces after its kind. Man is great because God is great. As intelligent as the ape species may be, I have yet to see any species as great as man.

Therefore, when I speak of the evolution of man, I speak to man's ability to grow, increase in capacity, and realize potential. Imagine having a car equipped with all of the bells and whistles and with the most modern technology, but all you do is start it and drive it from point A to point B. That would be a waste of money and a waste of a vehicle. What comforts and opportunities would be missed? The same is true of a life lived without realizing and tapping into one's potential. What a wasted life that would be?

**Awareness is the Beginning of Evolution**

The moment of awareness is the awakening. It is the moment where things begin to make sense. It is the moment the pieces of the puzzle called life assemble to make a clearer picture. The awakening is that monumental point of clarity. It is the convergence of time, experience, and opportunity that leads to purpose and destiny. The awakening is a moment that points to your *why*. In the moment of awakening, life takes on new meaning. Your focus is firm and distractions are diminished. To help reinforce this, I want to introduce Esther. I want to use Esther's story along with my own to help reinforce the notion of being the answer. What makes Esther so relatable is her background. In Beth Moore's *Breaking Free*, she suggests that God does not choose us in spite of our history. To the contrary, He chooses us because of our history.

You could be the answer and not be aware of it. Esther is a Jewish woman in the Bible whose experience many people can relate to. She had a tumultuous yet rewarding journey. And although intense, it was tempered with moments of great tranquility. Esther was chosen to be queen during her time and ended up becoming a heroine for the Jewish community. Esther was the answer. She was a savior for those whose lives were in jeopardy. The Jews were on a speeding train headed toward a collision course of destruction. Haman – an official of the King – set an all-out war against the Jewish community. Haman was able to get King Ahasuerus to sign a decree that all Jews would be killed within twelve months, on a specific day, all at one time. Yet, the answer that the Jews needed came from the most unlikely place, through Esther. She comes to the forefront as a savior and heroine. She went before the King and gets him to create another decree that would reverse what Haman initially put into place. She won! Her impact was so great that many Jews still celebrate her with a festive period observed every year called Purim. She would be a modern day from rags to riches story.

What is most intriguing about Esther's story is she never thought of herself as a savior, heroine, or even someone's answer. Esther was just glad be Queen. The same goes for me. It is amazing how people's view of you is very different than your view of yourself.

As you read this book, many of you cannot imagine with your life, your history, and your troubles that you are somebody's answer. But you are. H.M. Tomlinson said, "We see things not as they are, but as we are." Our life experiences helps to shape our view of self. In most instances, the more troubling and challenging life is, the harder it is to see your self-worth or capability of major feats. The hope Esther and I offer is a testimony on how your future is not controlled or restricted by your past. Additionally, we provide a comfort of knowing there are no wasted moments. Every experience – whether good, bad, or ugly – are all a part of those which become the arsenal for your future battles. You would not be *you* without them. One of our greatest challenges is not allowing bitterness to set in over adverse hardship – understanding that if God allowed it, He's in control. As difficult and disappointing my life experiences may have been, the best tool I garnered was the ability to change how I viewed them. I had to learn to view them in the light of my future destiny and not in the shadow of my past. I had to understand it takes all of what happened to make me. Every hurt, pain, failure, success, applaud, chastisement, loss, and gain were needed to create the James Nelson I am today.

When scientists are discovering a cure for disease or a creating serum to combat a plague, they have to be precise with the formula. One ingredient too much or one element left out changes the outcome and creates something new.

Let's use water for an example. Water is one oxygen atom bonded with two hydrogen atoms. If you add any other variation, you cease to have water. Two oxygen and one hydrogen doesn't result in water. While it will be something else, the result will not be water. When God created you as an answer, there was a specific sets of problems He had in mind for you to solve. It takes your genetic make-up to address those problems. There are specific problems that were designed to only be solved by *you*. Even when I was unaware that I was an answer, the specificity of the issue I was born to solve required certain elements to be used in the evolution of me. James and Bessie had to be the ones to create a James Jr., even though for years I fought and ran and lacked the cognition of who I was destined to be. Lack of awareness does not change being the answer. It simply means at some point – when the time is right – you have to be informed of who and what you are.

**Timing is Everything**

As revealed in the story of Esther, everything that happened to Esther was part of a formula to make her the answer that was needed in her time. The saying 'time is relative' is a descriptive statement made in judgement of the concept of time. Depending on where you are, how fast you are moving in relation to other objects, as well as the gravitational pull, time varies. Being aware of your role as an answer is only necessary when time calls for you to operate as *the answer*.

Esther had been married for five years before she became aware of who she was. Esther was a teenager when she married the Persian King Ahasuerus. It is suggested that she is as young as fourteen, as it was the custom and preference to marry younger women under eighteen. As a teenager, she is not concerned with being an answer. She is caught up in being chosen to be Queen and all that comes along with it after having such a rough life. She was an orphan adopted by her cousin Mordecai. Her father died while her mother was pregnant and her mother later died giving birth to her, leaving her orphaned. Can you imagine what it was like being Esther? Can you imagine the pain of growing up without both parents and possibly being the cause of one of their deaths? Now, can you imagine after such an arduous life being chosen to be Queen to a King over one of the most powerful kingdoms of all time? Esther had to have been thinking that this is the ultimate payback for the awful hand she had been dealt. How can a poor Jewish adoptee go from orphanage to being one of the most coveted women around? Esther had made it. Esther, you are finally there. Esther, you have what every woman would want. Little did Esther know, all of this was a part of being the answer. Now five years later, she finds herself having the demand of being a savior being placed on her. Everything is going great until Mordecai reaches out and says the magic words, "You are here for a time such as this." In essence, Mordecai was saying, 'You are not just Queen for vainglory, but you were made Queen to manifest your purpose.'

It is in this moment we see the role that time plays. Time is the key that brings awareness. The awakening is time sensitive. If it has not happened for you yet, do not panic. It simply means it is not time. Esther lived her life unknowingly carrying the solution to a problem that had not yet occurred. The answer is only relevant to the problem it solves. If there is not a problem, there is no answer needed.

As it relates to my own life, time was a major component I had to grapple with. I had to learn and understand every purpose has a time. I also had to accept my time would come when the purpose for which I was created was needed. A hard concept for me – and maybe still a little challenging – is waiting. "You never want anything before its time" is a truthful adage; however, the saying does not diminish the anxiety of waiting. Waiting increases in difficulty when you see the time for other answers happening. Waiting can make you question your relevance and purpose. Do I matter? What am I here for? Do I have anything to offer? The relativity of time can play on your emotional and mental stability. People have committed suicide during their waiting period. People have made grave missteps during this time, extending an already extensive wait. One reason I wrote this book was to help someone avoid the mistakes and missteps I made while waiting and being unaware of my identity. I want to make you acutely aware that YOU are an answer, whether the problem you are assigned to solve has emerged or not. Just give life time and you will see…You are the answer!

I am a son of a preacher. Out of the siblings, one of us were destined to follow in the family ministry and at the time a lot fell to me. Now, my entire family serves in some capacity of ministry. But back then, I was the preacher expected to follow in my father's footsteps. I have pastored my current church for over 10 years but this is not my first pastorate. I started pastoring my first church in the fall of 1999 on the Eastern Shore of Maryland in the small town of Cambridge. Cambridge is so small that if you don't pay attention while driving through, you could miss it. I was a city boy in a rural town pastoring a rural people. It was the best of times and the worst of times. Pastoring in Cambridge was one of the more challenging times in my life. I always dreamed of pastoring the church I grew up in, following after my father. However, my assignment at the time was in Cambridge and that did not end too well. I honestly felt like a failure as a pastor. I ended up leaving Cambridge during the winter of 2004, heading back to my family church and thinking my dream was about to come true. Little did I know, it would be the beginning of a series of happenings that would take me down to North Carolina and back again. When all was said and done, my brother Jason ended up pastoring the church, and I was left wondering *what about me?* It would be another four years before I would have an awakening that would bring me to my current assignment. Here is the take away, Destiny Christian Church – the church I currently pastor – could not manifest until the appointed time. The purpose and people Destiny would serve was not ready until spring 2008. Waiting is hard but timing is everything.

The good news is your time has come calling for the answers you possess. The answer you are is the perfect fit to meet the needs of others, to help squelch the noise of their beckoning problems. Esther had the answer to what had blossomed into a national crisis. Esther evolved to a place where she was able to respond appropriately to the situation at hand. Time works for us by guaranteeing we are ready for whatever the moment demands. All of the Jewish persons under the Persian government were due to be annihilated on the thirteenth day of the twelfth month. The King had made a decree and had the power to counteract it if he was made aware of the consequences from what was in motion. The real hero is not the King but the person who had the access and the ability to influence the King's decision. Esther was the only one. Esther was now ready to address a national crisis and only one thing hindered her – the fact that she did not know it.

**The Answer Realized**

Awakening is a moment of realization. Awakening is that moment where everything you have experienced, endured, and been exposed to comes together to paint a clear picture of *why*. Esther never thought of herself as the answer until the very moment she heard the words of Mordecai. When Mordecai said those words to her, it aroused something in her she never felt before. While being the answer has been commercialized and sensationalized, those who are the answer many times are left with a plethora of emotions. Overwhelmed, scared, excited, nervous, freaked-out, and flattered are just a fraction of some of the emotions felt when the moment of awakening comes. Am I ready for this? Is this really happening? How can I do this? These are some of the thoughts that can rush through your mind when awakening occurs.

Mary the mother of Jesus asked, "How could this be?" Gideon the mighty man of valor said, "You must have the wrong man because I am the least of my family." Even Jesus the Christ asked if there was any other way to save mankind and if the cup of taking on the sins of the world through crucifixion could pass from Him. That moment is unforgettable. That moment is intimidating. That moment is life changing when you realize your life really has meaning and purpose. Nothing is more thrilling than when all of the things you thought were wasted moments now in an instance of cohesion interlock to crystalize what purpose is for you. You are the answer!

What brings awakening is simple – a problem. Problems are problems for everyone unless you are the answer. To the answer, a problem is an opportunity. You have to be okay with the problem because the problem exposes the answer. The problem becomes the stage upon which the answer stands. The problem sheds light on the answer. Without the problem there would be no platform for the answer. It is the composition of the problem that determines the composition of the solution. The formula for the flu shot is determined by what makes up the flu. As a matter of fact, the flu vaccine actually consists of the inactivated flu virus. It takes a problem to create the solution. **What is wrong is really what is right.** I want to further develop this to bring clear understanding.

God always determines outcomes, ends, and answers before He does anything else. In God's mind, the answer precedes the problem. It is actually the answer that dictates the problem. For Esther, for you reading this, and for me, we were created to be the answer before we were born. Our purpose, the problems we would solve, and the lives we would impact were designed before the egg was fertilized in our mother's womb. The answer is not new. It has always been, but it has just been dormant. It is like Newton's law – an object at rest remains at rest unless acted upon by a greater force. The answer is inactive until what it solves comes to light. Therefore, God orchestrates what I call divine chaos with the single intent to awaken the answer. The chaos is controlled, the chaos is monitored, and the chaos is measured. It only has one purpose and that is to ignite the answer. That is how God arranges it. Nevertheless, to us, it is the reverse. The problem comes before the answer. It is the emergence of the problem that sheds light on the answer. Could it be possible that the very thing that frustrates and troubles us is the muse that awakens the answer within us? Could it be that our most difficult problem is really the catalyst to discovery of who you really are? The next difficult situation you face, the next time an issues rises at work, or that difficulty in your relationship is nothing more than an opportunity to discover and celebrate you being the answer.

This is what happened with Esther and what has taken place in my own life. The Jewish people having their lives threatened was simply the inspiration to Esther's moment of awakening. The problem became the incentive to see the answer she was. All of us have to have a moment of awakening, as did Esther. For Esther, it came when her cousin Mordecai made her aware of the national crisis that had arisen. Lives were on the line. A generation was being threatened. A whole ethnic group was in peril. But there was a much bigger picture. The lineage of Jesus would have been cut off, ultimately stopping the birth of our Savior. Jesus was a Jew and if all Jews were killed then there would be no Jesus. Esther not only saved the Jews but Esther saved Jesus. Who else are you saving by becoming the answer you were destined to be? I did not realize that hundreds of people who follow me every Sunday and thousands whom I preach to every year would not be impacted and helped if I did not come to the understanding that I am an answer.

Esther tried to avoid it at first. Esther did not want to accept it. She tried to run from it and push it off to someone else, but Mordecai let her know that she was in that position just for that purpose at that particular time. It was in that moment the light bulb went off. Picture if you will, the Queen with all her majesty sitting in a room full of people that suddenly becomes very small. All the voices are silenced and the conversations become pointless. All she hears is 'you are the only one who can fix this – it is all on you and you have to do this.' It was powerful and penetrating. It was exciting and intimidating. It was weighty. Esther understood that their lives depended on her.

# Chapter Four
## You Qualify

Steve Jobs took a concept, mastered it, and became an industry standard. Steve's intent was to be cutting edge and helpful by creating technology you could use to access the world from the palm of your hand. I will not use this book to promote my personal phone of choice, but the iPhone is by far one of the best on the market. The intent was to create better communication and convenience. In the last ten to twelve years, smartphones have revolutionized how people live. People almost cannot function without a cell phone. However, since the usage of mobile devices has increased, studies have shown interpersonal face-to-face communication has declined. This is especially true with the youth of today. Various studies have proven people to be more distracted during human engagement while phones are present. Cell phones have helped to foster an atmosphere of individuality and independence. People are more into themselves than before. You have answers, information, and connection at the tip of your fingertips, which has caused people to be less dependent on others and more into self. Being into self is not wrong but excessive independence can create a mindset that misaligns with reality. It can create a higher interpretation of self that may be unfounded.

For the sake of clarity, I endorse healthy self-perception as I have supported in earlier chapters, but one has to be careful not to portray something they are not. Having the ability to treat a wound or a medical issue does not make you a doctor. Knowing how to repair something pertaining to a car does not make you a mechanic. Putting out a fire does not make you a fire fighter. Having knowledge about a skill doesn't make you a master of it. There are steps or necessary qualifiers that affirm what you are or are not. Being the answer has qualifiers. Again, I stress I do believe everyone was designed to be someone's or something's answer, but you have to know what that someone or something is. The answer is specific. It is not a universal answer. The only person who was a universal answer was Jesus. I believe being the answer is targeted and focused, which adds to the value of the answer. That is what makes people compensate you and pay more for what you have because they cannot get it from anywhere else. When I was younger, my father told the story of a company whose machine stopped working. The in-house specialist did all they could to repair it. Finally, a mechanic was called in. He approached the machine and examined it. He proceeded to take out his hammer and hit the machine with one good pop. The machine started back up working just fine. The mechanic sent a bill for one hundred dollars. It read ten dollars for hitting the machine with a hammer and ninety dollars for knowing where to hit it. The moral of the story is the power of being the answer for a specific problem is what makes one invaluable. Companies will fight to keep you when you are the answer. People will respect you when you are the answer. Relationships will be healthier when you are the answer.

There are qualifiers for being the answer. The answer is only effective when addressing the problem they were created to solve. I believe the following five things can be a template to review when considering what you are the answer for. This checklist will help you to identify or disqualify a problem. There is no time or energy to waste. Effort has to match impact. You don't want to put effort into something for which you will have no impact. It is like pouring a single five-gallon bucket of water on a forest fire. There would be little to no impact. I want to help preserve your time.

Here are my five qualifiers:
1. You have <u>access</u> to what is beyond your reach;
2. You have <u>influence</u> that others do not have;
3. You have <u>capacity</u> others may not have;
4. You have <u>solutions</u> to specific problems; and
5. You have <u>power</u> that others do not possess.

Next, I will break each qualifier down to explain what they mean.

## Access

The first of these five qualifiers is access. The basic definition of access is entrance to, admittance to, a door, a passage, or inroads to something. Access is a powerful thing everyone wishes they had. Access is a key position and is only given to those who are trusted. Access means you have the ear of persons of power, affluence, and influence. For the national crisis at hand, the King had the power to address it but the common people, including Mordecai, did not have access or an inroads to the King. Esther was the only one with that degree of access to the King. She became a door for the Jews. Esther's access made way for the King to hear the issue at hand and give direction to counter and ultimately end the crisis.

Access is a tool to those who know how to use it but a weapon to those who abuse it. An important principle to remember for this qualifier is you only give access to those who can be trusted. Trust is earned. Character and consistency prove trustworthiness. Access is underrated in a society where everyone seeks to be the 'it' thing. In a self-centered world, access can be under appreciated. You do not have to be King when you have the ear of the King. Access to the King is just as powerful as being King itself. You can still get things done, you still have a position of prominence, and it can be just as rewarding. Access is a sign of validation. Access is a reward for faithfulness. The immature cannot handle certain levels of access. Once you give someone access and expose them to confidential information, you cannot take back what they learn.

Those with access understand the responsibility that comes with it and use it wisely. Esther does not just abuse her access but uses it wisely. What I have found is people with access can be mishandled and misused. Once a person knows who you have access to, they will use you to reach what they cannot do on their own.

Here is a note of personal experience. I have learned – as the answer – not to provide too much emotion or expectation to people who need my access. Remember, you are only an asset to them because you have passage to what they do not. You are a door for them to enter into their next. Do not attach emotions to being the answer. Being the answer that grants access is an assignment and a calling. I have been favored with access to many different groups, personalities, and entities and I am able to keep it because I guard it and I value it.

## Influence

Answers have influence connection and favor. Moreover, answers have the capacity to effect policy, people, and decisions. In our society of democracy, voter rights and electoral processes are important. For the candidates seeking to be elected, endorsements are priceless when it is from the right source. Having the right company or person endorse you can shift the outcome of the election. Lobbyist get paid big bucks because they help influence legislators to vote for specific bills and laws. Esther has favor and influence with the King. When she goes to the King, he extends to her the scepter which was a sign of favor, admittance, and acceptance. Queen Esther's presence, smile, and beauty affected the King to the point where he offered her half the kingdom.

What a great influencer she was? She did not abuse her power but used her influence to produce change and save lives. What are you willing to use your influence to accomplish? Who was the last person impacted by your influence? What good is having the ability to affect change but won't? The answer uses every resource God gives them to impact and bring solutions to whatever is ailing those you are called to serve.

## Capacity

Capacity is what many people lack. Capacity is more than a heart thing. I have come to know, learn, and appreciate some great people with big hearts but limited capacity. Capacity is aptitude. Capacity is the ability to produce. Capacity is the ability to house, maintain, and manage. Trust is not the same as capacity. I may trust you as my friend but not as my accountant. Your capacity to keep secrets and give great advice does not equate to the ability to count, manage, and oversee my fiscal affairs. The answer has capacity. It is what sets you apart. The good thing about capacity is it can be developed. An interesting thing concerning capacity is you really do not know the extent of your capacity until you put demand on it. Esther is not aware of the full extent of her capability until she was put in a place where demand was put on her. Mordecai reminded her of this. He told her she was brought to the kingdom for this and reminded her that she had the aptitude to handle a national crisis.

Challenges come to help us understand capacity. I did not think I had the ability to start a church from scratch, develop leaders, and cover other pastors. But all I experienced was stretching me and increasing my capacity. Every challenge was resistance to build the muscle of capacity. Resistance in body building is the catalyst for muscles being developed. I am glad I did not run when things went awry. I am thankful I did not allow people's behavior to cause me to quit. It was building me and strengthening my core. Embrace your challenge and be the answer you are destined to be.

## Solutions

You cannot be an answer without strategy. Solutions are a fix to strategies. Solutions are the basis of what the answer is. The answer is a 'fixer'. The answer is the Olivia Pope to whatever problem you are addressing. It is not just hoping something works, but it is methodically approaching a problem with a plan of action. Every move is calculated and intentional. It is like the game of chess – every single move is well thought out and tactical in nature. What qualifies you to be an answer is the ability to map out a distinct set of goals and a scheme to reach those goals. Esther was purposeful in her approach. Strategy implies pace. The answer must possess wisdom. Part of being strategic is having the soundness to know when to do what. Esther paces herself, even with the temptation of the King's offer and his impulses. She knows what to ask for, when to ask, and when to implement. The first thing Esther did was seek God for direction, divine favor, and His backing. She did not approach the King until her strategy was in place. Strategy keeps control. You will be okay if you just stick to the plan. God tells Joshua that he will have good success if he does not deviate away from the plan. The answer has nothing to prove. The answer cannot allow the pressure of their surroundings and the antsy nature of others to shift them from following the plan of action. Some of my greatest victories came through following a well thought out course of actions; and equally, most of my greatest defeats came from ill-timed, impulsive decisions.

A good strategy should include:

1. An analysis: This analysis overviews the current status of the environment, available resources, and the given situation. This will advise you of any threats and potential pitfalls.
2. A mission/vision/objective: What are you after and what do you desire to see as an outcome?
3. A timeline: Attach a time and date to every action.
4. An action outline: This is a detailed description of the necessary actions needed to achieve your intended goal.
5. A measurable assessment: This includes a thorough review of outcome effectiveness.

**Power**

The last of the qualifiers for the answer is power. Power includes authority, physical power, political power, and ability. This is not where you talk a good game but cannot perform. Power is physical strength to perform, but it is also authority to make things happen. Physical stamina is needed to keep up with the demands placed on being the answer. You have to be in shape mentally, emotionally, but especially physically. The demand of being the answer can wear you out and you have to be able to keep up. Next is the power of authority, which is the legal right to do, operate, and make decisions. If you allow, God will position you into a place of power. Elevation is not to sit high on the hog, as my father would say, but elevation is positioning to be in a place of authority to act.

Everything Esther endured was a set up to situate her in a place of authority to make moves. Joseph's trouble was nothing more than stairs to his ascension of power. Joseph ended up being second in command under Pharaoh. There was no one greater than Joseph in Egypt except Pharaoh. Where is God trying to place you to enable you to be the answer you were destined to be?

These are the qualifiers to be the answer. After reviewing these, you can see why Jesus was our answer. He possessed all five qualifiers. He had and gave access, was influential, had endless capacity, brought solutions, and had all power. Even though Jesus embodied all of these, do not allow yourself to become discouraged if you do not meet this criteria. You can have any combination of these to be the answer. And if you happen to not yet possess a certain qualifier, it could be an indicator that you are not the answer for that particular set of problems. Rest assured, you are more than qualified to address the problem that you are designed to be the answer to. You are the answer.

## Chapter Five
## The Responsibility of Being the Answer

To whom much is given, much is required and to whom much is entrusted, much will be asked. Everything comes with responsibility. The success we are blessed to experience, positions were are granted, and the affluence we are afforded all come with the weight of responsibility. We are familiar with the quotes 'Everything comes with a cost' and 'Nothing in life is free.' We get to enjoy those things, but some fail to acknowledge the baggage that comes with them. We have recently witnessed the fall of an entertainment icon. Bill Cosby was a household name and was America's father. He rose to a place of great power, influence, and fame. I do not bring this up for judgement or opinion, but simply as an observation that with great power – especially being an African American male – comes much accountability and responsibility. Those in power are held to a higher standard. Furthermore, those who are afforded various opportunities need to know that there is something required of them. Leadership – whether through mentoring or being an example – is required. Integrity and character is also required of them. These are just a few of the characteristics expected of those in these positions.

Most individuals want to 'make it' and succeed for selfish reasons. Some want it as an act of compensation for the struggle and sacrifice it took to get there. I will not say this mindset is wrong. I will say that when God opens a door, there is a twofold rationale behind it. First, according to the

Bible, God does make it up to us. The Bible is a book of God's word promises and thoughts toward us. One verse in Isaiah 61:7 says, "*Because you got a double dose of trouble and more than your share of contempt, your inheritance in the land will be doubled and your joy go on forever*" (MSG). God is sensitive to the suffering, pain, inconvenience, and trauma our process may cause. With God, it is always worth it. The secondary thought behind God placing us in these situations and affording opportunities is to position us to become effective answers.

## The Rules of Engagement

There was a national crisis at hand and the only person to arrest what was happening was Esther. Remember, she had the ear, favor, and heart of the King. She was chosen to be Queen. Vashti was the first Queen who lost her spot because she did not follow the direction of the King. She failed to follow the protocol for her position. I think it is important to note that every level, position, environment, and room has a protocol that accompanies it. Sometimes those protocols are known, and then other times there are unspoken protocols. There is a proverb that says 'It is better to be asked to come to the table then to sit at the table and be asked to leave'. To remain in the room, in that position, in that environment, and on that level, you must learn the protocol. It is not the responsibility of anyone to teach you. It is your responsibility to learn. It may not seem fair but that is the way of the world.

According to the military, the term Rules of Engagement (ROE) are the set of directives that define the circumstance, conditions, degree, and manner in which the use of force is applied during time of war. Since its initial use, the terms have been applied to sports, business, and even in dating. In the work place, ROE is the proper behavior of management and employees. The Rules of Engagement are protocols to follow. If you want to play the game then you need to know the rules of the game.

For Esther, she understood the rules of the game. She calculated the risk but understood this is what comes with the territory of being the answer. Being the answer may require risk, and according to the protocol of her time, no one came before the King unless invited. If you came before the King, you waited to see if the scepter was extended or not. A scepter was a type of ornamented staff carried by rulers as a symbol of sovereignty. An extended scepter meant you were accepted and a scepter that was not extended demonstrated displeasure and was punishable by death. Esther knew a nation was on the line. However, realizing that she was the answer, she went anyway and the scepter was extended in her favor.

As the answer, do not be afraid to learn the protocol for whatever level, room, business, or endeavor you desire to participate in. You learn protocol first by observation. Analyze and study where you aspire to go. Secondly, do not be afraid to ask questions from the right people. Third, seek out mentorship. Esther did all three. She had someone assigned to her so she could learn the ways of being a Queen.

She studied and learn from others' previous mistakes. Lastly, she had Mordecai as a voice of reason and as a mentor. Esther had success because she learned and followed the protocol established.

## It's Going to Cost You

We have had the privilege of witnessing various royal weddings, from Princess Diana and Charles, to Prince William, and even Prince Harry. Prince Harry's wedding caused a stir because the person whom he chose was neither British nor of royal descent. Meghan Markle was a normal American from Compton, California who became an actress. She met the prince through mutual acquaintance and they fell in love. After approval by the Queen, she and Harry married. This seems to be a fairy tale being played out before us. It is a rags to riches story inspiring all to believe in love, marriage, and happiness thereafter. It is the kind of tale that makes you feel all warm and fuzzy inside. Meghan's life will never be the same. She is wealthier than she could ever imagine, her popularity has soared, and the trajectory of her family lineage has shifted; notwithstanding, it came at a great price. Her father tried to extort her and use her newfound positioning and fame for his personal profit. She had to give up life as an actress, as well as her personal social media. She also has to live her life in public with no real privacy where everything she does is scrutinized. Many people want all of the glamourous things but do not want to pay the toll to access such a life.

Being the answer requires sacrifice, whether viewed from Esther's perspective or my own. Esther had to live as an adopted orphan. She had to sacrifice her comfort and the life she knew. She also sacrificed her safety by going before the King without invitation. Lastly, Esther sacrificed her serenity by taking on the task of saving a nation. For me, it was losing a childhood dream in order to embrace the will of God. It was painful and heartbreaking. I felt like I was being crushed. For a season, I did not have a dream at all. I found out that sometimes God has to break your heart to save your life. But when you are in it, you cannot see the daylight. It feels like it will never end, but it was all designed to position me to do what I am doing right now.

It is costly but if you ask Meghan, Esther, or myself, we would unanimously agree that it was well worth it. You have to see the cost as an investment and not as making a simple deposit into an ATM for an immediate return. Investments take time to maturate before you can access the return.

## It's Lonely at the Top

I am what some would call adventurous, especially in comparison to some of my contemporaries. I have a bucket list of things I want to accomplish. It is the thrill of conquering on the edge and the high of the adrenaline rush that gets the blood flowing and the heart racing. To me, this is living! This side of me has been there since I was a child. I was the boy climbing up trees and jumping off roof tops. Adventure is appealing to me. As a result, I find mountain climbing interesting. The thought of scaling rocks with rope and a few hooks dangling, hiking thousands of feet up above sea level and the ground peaks my curiosity. I must be honest, the closest I have come to accomplishing this was a good rock climbing wall. Don't judge me! I have noticed most climbers have a lot of support but the majority of the support remains at the base of the mountain. Whenever I have seen photos of those who made it to the top, it is usually only one person or just a few people. I have concluded for whatever reason, everybody does not make it to the top. If that is the principle, then as the answer you have to be okay with doing it alone. If everyone was an answer to the same problem, there would be no need for you or me. Being the answer calls for you to walk alone due to the access you are given. In the government, there are levels of access depending on your security clearance. When a person tries to access something beyond their salary range, they will be told that they do not possess the appropriate clearance for it. So many times we try to take people along for the journey that do not have the clearance for what we have been called to do.

Only the person who God has called to be the answer is expected to respond and go. Feeling like you do not fit in or feeling like an outsider are side effects of being the answer. David was left in the field by his brothers, Moses has to be raised in foster care, and Jesus went to His own but they did not accept Him. It's lonely at the top and you have to be okay with it. The good news is God graces and equips us to be the answer on our own. Now this is different than intentionally isolating yourself because you are going through or feel superior to others. This is understanding and accepting the cost. It's the assignment that separates you. Noah built an ark and no one believed it would rain. Abraham had to leave his father's country and family to begin a posterity never before established. The cost shows value. The more important, exclusive, and rare, the higher the cost. You are a rare precious commodity. You are the answer.

**Social Security**

In the cyber world one of the hot topics is cyber security. Identity theft is on the rise and personal information is liquidity. From the government and banking institutions, to fun personal sites, nothing seems to be off limits to cyber predators. There have been breaches leaking sensitive government information. Then there is the election of 2016 that will forever go down as one of the most controversial elections in history. There is more attention being given to the breach of cyber security than ever before. Companies brag in commercials that their security protocols are more efficient than any of their competitors. Congress grilled Mark Zuckerberg over the security of his clientele. Home security systems have outdone themselves to ensure family safety with some of the most advanced, high-tech gear. All this fuss for one thing – security. The most expensive and elaborate systems and protocols cannot provide security of self and individuality. None of those things can produce the security that comes from within.